The Alpha Point

A GLIMPSE OF GOD

By Anthony Strano

Illustrations by Manolo Galdon

THE ALPHA POINT

First Edition July 1998
Second Edition July 1999

ISBN 1-886872-13-9

Published by Brahma Kumaris Information Services Ltd, Publications.
Global Co-operation House, 65 Pound Lane, London NW10 2HH UK.

Author – Anthony Strano
Illustrator – Manolo Galdon

Printed by Elite Printing Co. Hong Kong.

This book has been produced by The Brahma Kumaris World Spiritual University,
a non-profit organisation, with the aim to share spiritual knowledge as a
community service for the personal growth of individuals.

The Brahma Kumaris World Spiritual University exists to serve the family of
humanity: to assist individuals to discover and experience their own spirituality
and personal growth; to understand the significance and consequences of
individual action and global interactions; and to reconnect and strengthen their
eternal relationship with the Supreme Soul, the spiritual parent.

http://www.bkwsu.com

Contents

Dedication

What Song can be sung

What Word can be spoken

What Act can be done

To give thanks to the One

Who has given me Existence

Who has given me Truth

Who has given the blessing of Eternity

Foreword

These writings on God are based on my personal experience of Raja Yoga as taught by the Brahma Kumaris Spiritual University. I can remember from a very young age, while growing up in Australia, that I wanted to know God in a real way. It was a silent search filled with readings of the Christian mystics, especially John of the Cross and Theresa of Avila, Julian of Norwich and, later on, readings of Buddhist and Chinese philosophy. At that time, it seemed that the more I read the less I knew. More and more I realised that silence and stillness are equally as important as knowledge. That is, as well as learning from the experiences of others, it was necessary for me to practise stillness. Not just praying, or chanting or reading, but coming into a state of deep inner silence in which the soul can listen to God. In stillness the soul can tune into aspects of being that exist beyond analysis and discussion. I knew I needed a method, a teaching on how to be still, silent, concentrating mind and heart on God.

Whilst coming to this realisation, I was introduced to the teachings of the Brahma Kumaris, which gave me deeper insights into spiritual knowledge, as well as methods of silence. Although I had been to India before starting Raja Yoga, I could not comprehend the many rituals, scriptures and the plethora of representations of God (especially the monkey and elephant gods!). Somehow I found it all too confusing and stayed clear of Indian religious philosophy, preferring to acquaint myself with Greek philosophy especially pre-theocratic, ancient mythologies and Christian teachings. However, in London, I heard a talk by the director of the Brahma Kumaris Spiritual University, Dadi Prakashmani, who was visiting from India. She said that the essence of effort to be with God is simply one word, Manmanabhav. This is translated in two ways: 'Remember one God', or that God says to the soul: 'Be mine with your mind'.

For me, that was it. I needed to learn from this university the simple way to experience the

Eternal One. So, I began with the Raja Yoga courses in London and now 20 years later, teaching Raja Yoga meditation in Greece, I am still experimenting with yoga and experiencing God. In this booklet I have shared my feelings about some of the relationships one can experience with God. Certainly, there are others – the rest for another time, another booklet.

I hope that you use my essays as a springboard for your own yoga experiments, and that you come closer and closer to the loving heart of God.

All the best,

Anthony

The Alpha Point

"All reality lies in the point"

PYTHAGOREAN SCHOOL

Imagine a huge, unlimited space far beyond this world of time, matter and action: a world of golden silence; not a drop of sound; no hands of time directing existence; a land of permanent peace and freedom. This is the world of eternity: silent and unchanging. In this world lives a point of conscient energy, eternally bodiless; a pure being who calls this world 'Home'. This point of pure, benevolent and all-knowing energy radiates light. This is the Alpha Point. This is God.

Alpha, silent and incognito, is the Beginning, the Seed, the Source, the Original One. This Benevolent Being is the eternal reference point for human life within which exist the qualities we need for elevating our life.

Living in this soundless and peaceful world, Alpha is the only Being who is beyond the process of change and decay to which we are all subject here on earth. Though beyond our world of matter, and forever incorporeal, Alpha does enter this world of time and sound, at the moment when negativity reaches its extreme. He enters to donate His life force, the divine energy of His being, to restore humanity and nature to its original state of harmony and order.

Without ever becoming human Himself, Alpha enters this physical world, playing His role and achieving the task of renewal through certain human souls. The most important is the one who is historically remembered as Adam, the first man.

In ancient Greece it was said that the Creator takes hold of the creation when it reaches a point of complete degradation and disorder. The creation is then cleansed and released, to move on its own natural course till a full cycle is completed. At the end of this cycle, when there is total decay and disorder, the Creator once again takes hold of the creation, cleanses it and lets it go. This repetitive process of taking, cleansing and letting go was called the eternal rhythm of the universe; a rhythm expressed continuously through never-ending cycles of time. Time itself was called the moving image of eternity and eternity was represented by a circle.

In India, in the Bhagwad Gita, it is said that God comes at the time of greatest degradation, when everything is in complete disorder and imbalance. He comes especially to restore and rejuvenate the original order of all things.

In many myths and legends different cultures have spoken of a time of degeneration when the earth falls into complete chaos and then order is restored through divine intervention. A Supreme Being is shown acting as the one who harmonises and sustains life.

The cycle of human life begins with the Alpha Point, goes full circle and then must return to the point of the beginning. The end and the beginning meet in Alpha, and through this eternal meeting there is purification and renewal.

The Alpha Point, who can be called God, Creator or Supreme Soul, is complete and self-sufficient. His power is unlimited and, in this sense, infinite, so no matter how much of His energy is given for this renewal it never diminishes in any way.

The Supreme Soul, being a point of conscient energy, is not present everywhere. However, from His home of silent light, His thought can reach everyone, everywhere, at any time. He is indivisible, independent and individual – not omnipresent or divided into parts. He is eternally a point who radiates to all and is close to all through the power of His love.

His identity is unique. He is who He is. His identity and the role He plays are permanent. A human soul cannot become God, can never merge with or become part of God, but we can become like God. The strong, sweet energy of Alpha can be absorbed by the soul, creating a union of deep bliss. It is such a union that transforms the soul.

One principle of Life is eternal individuality. Each soul, including the Supreme Soul, is unique. Uniqueness gives each being its special value, a value which is innate and imperishable. It is this difference that creates the beauty of life. Difference does not cancel feelings of harmony and closeness; in fact, difference enhances those feelings.

Alpha is only One and will always be One, in the same way as there is only one of me and one of you.

The play of life on earth is made possible only because each actor is unique; each one of us has his own part, as does God. Like the fingers of a hand which are all different, but must function together so that they can be called 'hand', true harmony is only possible when we appreciate the differences and unite on the basis of respect. There is never the need to go beyond our unique differences to advance oneness. On the contrary, to respect and appreciate difference becomes the true method for creating oneness.

This oneness, this unity, becomes a reality through selfless love. Love that is pure allows us to feel at one with each other. As a global family we need to feel such empathy.

The Alpha Point is unique. He is the absolute and eternal Good and the closer we move towards that absolute, the more we can absorb that pure goodness. This is the basis of personal transformation and of awakening the eternal uniqueness of the self.

Deep silence is required. Through that gentle concentrated silence we can experience all relationships with God, the eternal and conscient energy.

Relationships

"We must not just think about God,
we must concentrate on Him;
to think about creates theology,
to concentrate on creates relationship.
Only relationship brings experience"

Relationship is a mingling of essence, a fusion of being, an integration of similarity; and especially, it is a friendship based and built on the vision of equality and love, love which constantly adds to the sense of self-worth.

Relationship is friendship, a friendship that not only adds but shares, multiplies and sustains the best. It never subtracts or empties because there is too much respect to allow such a thing to happen. A true relationship honours the individuality of the other's existence, so consequently there is not a speck of degradation as a result of attachment.

A love-filled relationship is the deepest desire in the human soul. Its experience and expression give meaning and fulfilment to life. Such a relationship inspires us to reach the highest happiness and to develop our deepest potential.

On the other hand, if relationship is tainted by selfishness, it can become a great source of pain, wounding with fear and despair. Whether a relationship gives happiness or pain depends on how much selfishness there is.

When a relationship is selfless, there is a natural feeling of contentment, of being truly alive. This is how real love works. When you ask people what love is, they often cannot express it in words, though everyone has experienced it to one degree or another. When love is real, we behave naturally, without calculating and without measuring. There is no need to appease or analyse. Everything falls into place by itself.

To keep a relationship real we don't need to labour. What we do need is to be honest with ourselves and each other.

God loves us as we are and for the individuals that we are. He loves us simply because we exist. The only prerequisite is that we are clear and honest with Him. God is not someone to bargain with or order around. He listens, understands and helps without wanting anything for himself. This is what a true friend does and He is our best and most faithful friend.

A relationship, whether with God or a fellow human being, needs caring and regard in order to maintain its freshness, its spontaneity, its worth. A relationship is always in danger of becoming uninteresting and routine, until we make a real commitment.

Love that is genuine cannot be bought, sold or bargained for. It can only exist if it is freely given. Likewise, a relationship is only true when it is freely chosen and it only functions when it is not exploitative. Unfortunately, over the centuries, the relationship between God and the human being has often been imposed upon people by organised religions. It is this man-made imposition that has led to misconceptions and negative feelings about God. Instead of a being we can be close to, we have imagined a vengeful God of fear and punishment. God is an eternally pure being and a pure being could never commit the violent retribution we have been taught to expect.

Whether the arena is religious, social or political, it is people in roles of authority who often exploit the needs of the masses to gain position and power, rather than serving them. When this happens, the result is always violence. It is people who sometimes cover up their own insecurities by highlighting the weaknesses or mistakes of others. It is people who manipulate emotions to make others feel guilt for what they have done, or not done, or even, simply, for what they are. All of these are different kinds of violence and all of these come from human beings, not from God.

There is truth in the expression 'God is Love'. Love only expresses the positive. It never focuses on what is wrong, but on what is intrinsically good in a person. Love has the power to defuse negativity.

When there is love, there is no desire to compete with or dominate the other because, in a way, the other is myself. How I value the other is the mirror of how I value myself.

Love creates a constant respect for all things. Love without respect degenerates into expedience. Honour is lost.

God honours each of us. Where there is sincere love, misunderstandings will not happen. When there are mistakes or failures, there is no need for constant regret, no need to keep asking for forgiveness. We have already been forgiven.

The problem is we cannot forgive ourselves. Lasting self-forgiveness is only possible when we change the things we do which rob us of our self-respect.

A relationship with God is never a dependency. It is not coloured by owning, demanding or expecting. It never makes us feel inadequate if we do not live up to expectation. God has faith in our potential.

He frees us, making us independent. This independence comes when we find our spiritual identity. We learn to have faith in what we are and the courage to realise it. Spiritual independence never breeds arrogance. It always keeps us close to one another.

Love generates trust and trust is the heart of a relationship. Trust comes from knowing that this relationship, this friendship, has permanency. It is a commitment.

Love maintains loyalty. Loyalty is the result of each of us seeing the worth of the other. Loyalty comes when there is a willingness to grow together, when we learn to accept any limitation and use it as a springboard to generosity. Generosity overlooks weakness and keeps our vision on the other's true self.

God as the
Father and Mother

*"In the Universe the eternal principle is Love.
Forgiveness and tolerance are the values born from
love. Forgiveness and tolerance are the hands of God
in action. We need to join our hands with God's to
learn and do the same"*

God is not just a point, He is not just energy. God is a conscious living being and what is conscious and living has personality. Personality includes the capacity to create feelings, form relationships and to play a role in the drama of life.

One key relationship that God has with His creation is as the eternal Mother and Father. In this relationship are combined the eternal masculine and feminine principles which give life and sustenance.

The eternal Father, out of His love, creates new life. He has the power to renew and to reorder the universe. Through Truth He establishes harmony and wellbeing. Like the physical sun, the masculine principle is still, fixed, full of power radiating light. This constant light is the energy that creates life.

As the eternal Mother, God cares for and patiently nourishes with encouragement and selfless love. The eternal Feminine, like the physical earth, is ever giving, renewing and nurturing. God, as the eternal point of reference, is fixed in form, position and role, but His energy gently and powerfully awakens and sustains.

In reality, all human souls have the eternal principles of the Masculine and Feminine but, according to time, one is emphasised more than the other.

God, the eternally incorporeal Soul, has these eternal principles within Himself also, but He never takes a physical form. God expresses the masculine and feminine qualities through subtle energy.

When the mind and heart are concentrated on God, then the human being can feel the Fatherhood and Motherhood of God – that is, the love, the power and the nourishment.

God's primary role is to create. The creating is characteristic of the eternal masculine principle, which is probably why in many religions God is referred to as the Father.

One aspect of his creating is to awaken His children from the deep sleep of forgetfulness. God sends energy and power in the form of pure thought, helping us to remember our original nature, peaceful and free. It has been said that the definition of truth is to remember what you have forgotten. So the Father awakens our remembrance so that we can become peaceful and free once again. This awakening is from the conscious limitations of the physical world. This allows us to perceive the horizon of the spiritual world.

God is the universal Father and Mother of all. He Himself is not a Hindu, a Christian, a Buddhist or a Muslim, for religions, though divinely inspired, are made in this world. God

Himself is not a Christian, a yogi or a Buddhist, but He loves them equally and belongs to them all.

God has the power to belong to all because he loves and understands all. To the extent that He is powerful, He is gentle. True spiritual strength always demonstrates itself in gentleness and respect. God would never use force or impose His will. No relationship, especially one with God, can develop, or even really begin, if there is force, because force is violence. Any violence, whether against ourselves or others, violates dignity.

The greatest example of such violation is when people or groups of people use force in the name of God to justify their own personal aims, and call it God's will or God's law.

The use of violence, physical or emotional, against the will or choice of others indicates not only lack of respect but overwhelming insecurity. To force another to believe what we believe, to do as we do, to think as we think underlies our inability to be free and independent and to understand and respect ourselves.

The Father respects the eternal individuality of each of us. We are souls, each unique and valuable, and from a spiritual perspective we are equal. Whether we are men or women, whether we are from different cultures or countries, no matter what our religion, we are primarily spiritual beings. When we live with this vision of equality, it is very easy to appreciate, accept and encourage our differences.

God, as the eternal Mother, loves us unconditionally and, as the Mother especially, forgives. With forgiveness a child is encouraged to learn from mistakes and to go beyond them. If we identify with our mistakes or failures we cannot learn from them. Instead we develop negative attitudes such as self-pity and guilt. We lose respect for ourselves. Most of us find it hard to forgive ourselves, and when the Father's unlimited love is not understood and we cannot forgive ourselves, we feel almost an obligation to suffer because we feel we don't deserve to be happy.

Our thoughts turn in on themselves and we begin to believe that, somehow, the more we suffer, the worthier we become. We actually believe that God sends suffering to those He loves! This tangled thread of thought needs to be unravelled, for the sake of our own happiness and peace of mind. Our inheritance from God is happiness, not suffering. Real love cannot give suffering.

God is our loving Father and Mother and gives all the strength we need to overcome the effects of mistakes. However, until we take up the personal responsibility of examining and changing ourselves, we build an unconscious barrier against God's love – a love that can miraculously heal.

God is working for our happiness. Our Father is the Ocean of Happiness, not the Ocean of Sorrow.

God's gift as the eternal Parent is to release us from suffering. Love gives us the strength. With the support of divine love we have no fear of mistakes and none of the pressure of expectations.

For many people, the negative image of God as the one who judges and punishes interferes in their relationship with Him. This negative image can be very deep in many people, depending on their social tradition and upbringing. So, often, there is automatic rejection when the name 'God' is mentioned. The negative reactions usually centre around words like 'punishment', 'hell', 'repentance', 'sin'. We require a new understanding and a new image of God. If we begin to think positively about God we will find a new relationship with Him, a new way of understanding this supreme, loving Being.

We need to begin to understand that God as a Being of Eternal Goodness must hold positive qualities, not negative ones. It is like our perception of people: if we hold on to a negative vision of them, if we keep this in our consciousness, then our relationship with them cannot improve and nothing will change. We keep confirming our own negative viewpoint because we see what we expect to see. Our preset conditioning gets stronger with each encounter and we cannot break out of the negative trap we've created. The relationship is doomed.

In order to change old attitudes and to break from our conditioning, we need to step back from the past, from what we've been told and, most especially, from what we think we know. We need to be a little detached from ourselves. To make effective changes we should look for the positive in others and, of course, in ourselves. So many books have been written emphasising the fact that self-healing and better relationships begin with our own, positive vision. We are exhorted to 'Look for the positive in everything'. This also should be our attitude towards God.

In silence we can gradually create a loving link with God. When we give time to silence and to reflection we can begin to feel God as the Father and Mother coming closer and closer. There is such a sweetness in this experience that the soul begins to open like a flower in the warmth of the sun. This closeness, this communion with God, has been experienced by many people in different cultures throughout history. For example, Christ called God 'Abba', a word used by young children for their father expressing trust and confidence in his love. In India, the people say of God: 'You are the Mother, you are the Father' and often God is called 'Baba', a term of great affection and regard.

God as the Father is Truth and as the Mother, Love. The combined qualities of these two roles create the imperishable sweetness of God. God is sweet. Sweet in the sense of being gentle, kind and good. Such sweetness is a sign of spiritual power. Unfortunately, emphasis on 'repentance', 'hell' and 'punishment' have obliterated our sense of God's inherent goodness, His caring and His sweetness.

The ancient people of Egypt particularly remembered God in terms of Love and Truth and as the Lord of Sweetness. Their feeling of closeness can be seen from this ancient prayer to Ra, their sun god.

Hail to thee, Ra, Lord of Truth,

whose sanctuary is hidden, Lord of gods...

who hears the prayer of him

who is in captivity

who is kindly of heart when

one calls upon him,

who saves the weak from the strong,

the humble from the proud,

for love of whom the Nile comes

Lord of Sweetness, great in love,

at whose coming the people live.

The Teacher: the Lord of Nectar

Wise is the one who, on hearing spiritual knowledge, has the courage to put it into practice – daily and consistently. Knowledge is transformed into wisdom when there is a commitment to learning. Learning means change. Knowledge alone can simply remain as entertainment for the mind. It can please our ears or astonish us with the clever acrobatics of words. When this is all there is, there is a great poverty of spirit. This expresses itself in both a lack of direction and a lack of contentment. For knowledge to be more than just stored information, we need to use it for change. Without change there is no benefit.

There are three degrees of change: one is simple change itself; another is the development and progress of the soul; and the deepest and most dramatic is transformation, complete metamorphosis. Change can be effected through positive thoughts which help us create positive attitudes. A change towards the positive helps us to live life fully. We become better people. Any individual who truly decides to can change something within. We all have enough inner strength to choose at least some ways of living that are more beneficial to us. The only real barrier is that the level of our effort is not deep enough to effect a lasting change. What is comfortable and convenient tends to take precedence over what is necessary.

For the soul to progress in spiritual terms, it needs change that is so deep that spiritual power is required for its permanent achievement. There are deeply embedded habits and patterns that cannot be changed just through being positive or having understanding. Deeper processes are required. For this we must learn to use our own soul energy, together with the divine energy of God. With this double strength we are able to change old negative patterns completely. This kind of change can be permanent.

Empowered, we are able to cope successfully with external difficulties. Inwardly, there is stability and strength, so the seeds of negativity cannot take root again. The transformed person is able to sense the shadow of negativity before it takes hold and stop it before it deludes the soul and causes damage.

The next stage is metamorphosis. Change can make one a better person and the right kind of progress makes one more spiritual, but metamorphosis actually makes the soul divine. Metamorphosis is the process of absolute and complete transformation – so much so that the human being is no longer recognised to be human. A total renaissance of the intellect occurs and, through this, there is complete restructuring of spirit. Many have called this renaissance of the intellect 'the opening of the third eye'. It is understood to be a superhuman leap in consciousness. The deeper one moves into the self, the higher the leap.

To understand the process of metamorphosis, we can look at the example of the ugly, heavy, earth-bound caterpillar, with its many legs, crawling everywhere, constantly eating. In time, it spins its home and in that cocoon silently hides itself away from the eyes of the world as Nature does her incognito work. In silence metamorphosis takes place. Then one day a totally new creature emerges from the cocoon. No longer earth-bound, its legs have disappeared. Now, wings brightly painted, it sails through the sky, stopping from time to time to sip nectar from the flowers. The wonder of this metamorphosis is a miracle we have come to accept as ordinary.

A human being deeply touched by God's love makes the journey deep into introspective silence. In that silence the soul remembers God and, in that remembrance, weaves the cocoon of human metamorphosis. The One who is pure Truth nourishes the human soul with love, as it transforms.

In India God is given the name Somnath, the Lord of Nectar. The nectar that makes the soul immortal is this Truth. In Greece, the gods of ancient myth are remembered as living only on ambrosia, the sacred nectar which kept them immortal. Many stories and myths are symbols of deeper truths. The gods symbolise the soul of human beings – by nature, immortal. The life of the soul can only be sustained by the non-physical – that is, by the subtle energy of truth. The human soul cannot be sustained by physical external things such as money, position, fame. These things, though plentiful, starve the soul. To return to its immortal identity, what we call self-realisation, the soul requires subtle, non-physical food as well as relationship with the non-physical being, the Lord of Nectar.

To commit one's self to spiritual perfection we need to return to our original consciousness of being a soul, an immortal spiritual being. Only God can teach and guide us in our return to spiritual essence. The ambrosia of Truth enters our intellects, putting a brake on our habit of creating the wasteful and the negative. With accurate understanding and consistent practice, truth becomes wisdom. Without practice there cannot be transformation. In reflective silence, and with our companion, the Supreme Teacher, we are given the courage and patience for total change.

Every day, especially in the early morning before human minds awake and the traffic of their thoughts and words congest the atmosphere, the spiritual effort-maker awakes to greet the Lord of Nectar. In that pure stillness, just before dawn, the soul is filled with the sacred energy so necessary for the spiritual journey.

It is the time to absorb deep into the self the ambrosia of the Divine for at that time God's loving vision is especially strength and clarity.

The one who remains the loyal companion of the Teacher experiences the most miraculous transformation of all. Eventually the human soul emerges from the cocoon of silence, more than human, a being of light, with a body of subtle energy. The soul can fly with the power of thought. It can fly anywhere as the messenger of God. This is the angel. Through God impossible things become possible. This type of transformation requires a total focus on the eternally True One, a focus practised each day of our lives. There is a phrase for this process of focused, unwavering thought. Manmanabhav means 'Remember only Me' or 'Be Mine with your mind'.

When we remain intent on achieving spiritual realisation, our hearts and our minds constantly with God, the relationship deepens and it becomes natural to be distracted no longer.

We are all given the same opportunity by the Supreme Teacher, but it is our responsibility to make the choices that will determine our level of achievement.

God is truly democratic. A teacher gives the same lesson to all the students. His duty is to explain clearly and patiently, giving extra explanations and time where it is needed, but ultimately the result depends on the effort of the student.

For the student to be successful there has to be humility. A humble student is willing to learn. The greatest obstacle to spiritual endeavour is arrogance. Arrogance totally blocks the capacity to learn effectively. The arrogant intellect says: 'I know', 'I know enough', 'I don't need this lesson', 'I've heard this before', 'You're the one who needs to learn this; I already know it'. Such thoughts dwarf our capacity to realise that learning is a life-long process and we never stop being students in this classroom of life.

The Supreme Teacher teaches with equality. He has no favourites. It is simply that those who accept the responsibility for their own self-transformation, those whose deepest desire is to learn from the Supreme Teacher, find that the lines of communication between the Teacher and the student quickly open. With no barriers to understanding, God's constant response can be felt.

Such true students, in time, become masters. Masters are those whose accumulated experience of learning and living has become wisdom.

Knowledge is the bridge to this wisdom. If we stand on the bridge without crossing over, if we content ourselves with just looking at the other side, we begin to believe that seeing is the same as knowing. Then we theorise, philosophise and continue in the comfort of speculation. Speculation is comfortable, because the one who remains on the bridge does not have to commit himself in any direction. Sometimes these are the very people who become confused and upset about small things and go to pieces when situations are really difficult.

Silence is the most important part of the learning process. Talking, reading and searching are not enough. It is inspirational to hold ideals, to search and to discuss, but the commitment truly to change means we need the courage not to remain comfortable. Closeness to the Supreme Teacher is the real inspiration for our own personal change. His truth is the basis and the compass for humanity's highest ideals.

Throughout human history such truth in the form of ideas and teachings appears, disappears and appears once again. When the eternal truths fade from human consciousness then a time of crisis always ensues. Crises signal the necessity to re-evaluate our lives and offer the opportunity to change. Crises, no matter how extreme, herald new beginnings.

Since Truth is eternal, enlightened ideas are recycled through time, in different cultures and in different periods, appearing and disappearing according to necessity. In history, when eternal Truth returns, it is always experienced as though it were new. Its reappearance stimulates new insights and perceptions.

Humanity's Truth is that, in time, it forgets again. This forgetting is the result of hearing about or talking about Truth, but not practising it.

The role of the beloved Teacher is to inspire the remembrance of the eternal Truths, which restore authenticity in life. These restore the quality of living. This resurrection of the spirit is possible through remembrance. It is not a matter of ritual or sound, but of connection with the Father. This loving, silent connection enables the human soul to transform step by step, day by day.

The True Guide: the Satguru

The true Guide shows the ultimate destination – freedom. Only one who is completely free himself has the capacity to liberate. That One can only be God.

This is a freedom which is not won by any physical revolution nor by any social or political strategy, but through undivided attention on the One. Through inner attentiveness the soul is given the strength and the insight to know itself. This knowing separates the artificial from the real within ourselves. The divine strength of the Guide enables us to conquer the artificial – the part of us that creates insecurities, fears, possessiveness and ego. Victory over the artificial self revolutionises personality. Victory is when we become self-aware, soul-conscious. In consequence the mind is disarmed, disarmed of negativity, waste, and evil. Disarming the mind gives peace and sweetness to our words, thus helping to build the bridge of communication.

History tells us of many revolutions and revolutionaries wanting to be free, but on the spiritual path it is only the inner revolution, that total reorientation of consciousness, that generates a freedom which is permanent and unaffected by anyone or anything external.

On the path to liberation we have to be spiritually authentic otherwise we simply will not survive, let alone succeed. Our level of spiritual authenticity is directly linked to our level of obedience. Obedience to the True Guide guarantees not only our survival, but our victory. That One is God. I need my guidance from Him. No human being can play that role, because no human being is beyond sin. Sin is the betrayal of Truth for selfish objectives. A spiritual guide, whose teachings are tainted with selfish objectives, can be an impediment to the attainment of another's spiritual destiny. The True Guide gives us unequivocal freedom. Everything else is secondary.

Spirituality must be a personal choice and must never be a result of obligation. True spirituality is freedom and freedom for ourselves can only be found through the True Guide. Through His wise guidance we are given a mirror and, in His silent sweetness, we face ourselves. It is no small victory to face the self and win.

There is a painting of the victorious archangel Michael holding a set of scales in one hand and a sword in the other. He is thrusting the devil away from himself. Michael is full of light, beautiful and clear. The devil, Satan, is filled with darkness, ugly and crumpled. The unusual thing about the painting is that the features of Michael and those of the devil are exactly the same. It seems clear that these represent not two different souls, but two aspects of the same soul. The devil symbolises the negative, while the angel symbolises the original and divine.

We create our victory by the internal effort of freeing the self from the self, the false from the real. To do this we need knowledge, symbolised in the painting by the sword, and have balance, symbolised by the scales. Balance means not going to extremes about anything, even for the good. So we need to balance silence with words, observation with action and determination with flexibility. Knowing when to do what is necessary for self-progress. Knowing when to do what comes from the connection with God, the True Guide and Satguru.

Like the painting of Michael, angels always keep their connection with God, the Satguru, whether fighting the devil or serving humanity. And while the devil or Satan is symbolic, God is not. God is the absolute Good and He, as the absolute good, has no opposites. Satan is symbolic of our own impurities. Impurities are the result of choices that are wrong and the resulting negative consequences over time. The habits of negativity have become so deeply embedded in the soul that we definitely require the assistance of God to guide us out of this labyrinth.

A real connection with God, the Satguru, is best when we give our hearts and minds to Him unconditionally. This closeness allows the possibility of complete victory over ourselves.

What does it mean when we say that the Satguru gives us freedom? Freedom is independence. In independence we can express ourselves and share with each other but there is no need in our relationships. Need creates demands and expectations and so limits the freedom of others. Need is a constant source of pressure in our lives.

When we are independent, we are the masters of ourselves. One major characteristic of natural or spiritual independence is a loving nature – a spirit of generosity that enables one to go beyond the weaknesses of others.

A truly liberated person is self-reliant, but never lets this turn into arrogance. Such a person is unique without being egocentric and open-minded without losing the power of discernment. The liberated person is certain without being dogmatic and has a true humility that never degenerates into subservience. There is always courage, but never the false intoxication of recklessness and, though courageous, the person treats life with care. Such a soul is both a master and a child, at the right time, a leader who has maturity enough to know when it is time to listen and follow.

A liberated person is one who trusts without fear of being deceived, who believes that when there is honesty, the Universe will give protection, that its laws are such that even if others misuse that trust he or she cannot lose. Experience teaches us to be careful the next time but still, even then, we can trust. Although aware of negative possibilities we keep our faith in life. Without this we become constantly suspicious, even bitter, and our fear keeps us from really living our lives.

Spirituality is the day-to-day liberation of the mind from its many dependencies. Though many people may prefer their dependency to freedom, consciously they would vehemently deny this. Even though dependency can be painful, it is at the same time comfortable. So, if we put up with something or someone disagreeable because of dependency, we avoid what we really have to do. We distract ourselves from the real issue by inventing plausible explanations and we try surface solutions which never work. This is why the pain, the disappointment and the emptiness do not go away.

When people are dependent, they are like birds in a neat and tidy golden cage, where their mutual support, though comforting, actually keeps them trapped. As the saying goes: 'Birds of a feather flock together'! They sing one particular song and the lyrics are 'blame, complain and compare'. Their lives function on the basis of these three words. They never lose the tune and never forget the words, always finding something, someone or some circumstance to sing about. Never looking into themselves, they never realise their own potential to go beyond their self-imposed limits, to be free. They never realise that they themselves are the ones who give power to negative situations and who make other people and other situations their masters.

They fly around and around in their circular cage of limitations, sometimes feeling the frustration of these limits and complaining about them, but rarely realising that they have created their own cages. After all, a cage can be convenient and comfortable and, above all, it is familiar.

The less people look inward, the more they look outward, projecting responsibility onto others. Every projection creates another bar to the cage. The key to this cage is always within reach, for it is inside. When someone acknowledges the personal potential for freedom and finds and uses the key to leave the cage, it is called enlightenment. Enlightenment is nothing more than realizing where the key is.

To believe in the key and use it requires assistance. The only assistance that is truly altruistic is given by God, the true Guide. He encourages us as we go inside to meet ourselves. The Guide gives the power to be free. What we have to do is constantly to hold the thought of freedom and be true to ourselves. He does the rest.

The Satguru leads us, not only into remembrance, but also into the experience of our original purity, the state of complete independence. This is the return to our original dignity. This return to dignity gives value to life.

We turn the key and we fly out of the cage. To fly is to have a new vision of our lives and ourselves – new attitudes that do not bind us to comfortable irrelevancies. The Guide gives the soul the wings to fly beyond the gravity of old patterns. A mind that is filled with animosity, a mind that cannot forget the past of others, a mind busy in self-justification cannot see the original goodness that exists in life. To raise ourselves beyond the gravity of routine and ritual, we have to believe in the best. We have to believe that within the chaos of present life there still lives the seed of our original goodness, waiting to grow again.

God focuses His attention on the original good within us. That seed of goodness cannot be obliterated by any negativity. Not only does He maintain this positive focus, but He teaches us to do the same. This eventually enables us to realise our potential and brings out our best.

Happiness is not possible without freedom. Hence, the necessity for God. Only non-material energy can penetrate the patterns, dissolve them and liberate the soul.

We must come close and know God for this to happen. It is false humility to say that God is too great, too pure to come close to. No matter what mistakes a child makes, the love of the Father and Mother never ceases. Love accepts us as we are, love unites. Love never rejects or distances itself for any reason. Those who think it does have not really understood the love of God.

As the Satguru, God guides our every step towards freedom. He teaches us the laws of the universe, the eternal laws of truth that maintain harmony and well-being. Even God Himself is obedient to these eternal laws. He works by them, He flows with them, because these laws preserve harmony and order.

To the Satguru, who holds these laws within Himself, we are obedient. When we understand the truth and the necessity of these laws, we naturally follow them and, in so doing, we maintain the rights of the self and others to be happy and free. In essence the laws centre on respect, a respect that maintains the dignity of all things. If we behave without respect for others, it is a debt in our spiritual account which at some time will have to be paid back. This debt means a loss of personal happiness.

Respect is the principal value that emanates from Love. Through the respect of others we gain liberation. The ultimate liberation is to live with matter and in relationships without dependency and without causing any imbalance or violence either to people or nature. Independence of being is only possible through soul-consciousness and this spiritual consciousness maintains the freedom and dignity of everyone, and keeps us close and loving to others.

Sometimes people think that, on the spiritual path, true liberation is to leave the world and its people totally. However, true liberty is not to reject the world as negative or illusionary but to see it as it is, to live in it and to change it where we can, through our spiritual consciousness.

Many things are not wrong in themselves but their use is wrong, because the consciousness behind that use is selfish. For example, there is nothing wrong with money or science but, when there is greed, ego, or fear, then these things are used incorrectly. So it is not anything in particular that we have to renounce, but our way of thinking about it. The renunciation of our thoughts is a far more difficult thing than the renunciation of an object or another person. Renunciation of thought is far more subtle, because our thoughts are intrinsic to our being.

We create our cages through our own thoughts and desires. Such desires create needs and dependencies and these bring about imbalance. Individuals who are truly free have eliminated destructive patterns from their lives. Freedom means to live in peace – to be totally non-violent. It is not necessary to be a saint or a sage to achieve this. It is only necessary to be a true human being.

A human being becomes true through interaction with the One who is Truth. This interaction elevates consciousness to the natural state of purity. Purity is the soul expressing itself through matter, harmoniously and non-violently.

God as the Beloved

The aim of nearly all human beings is to find their other half, another person who will make them complete, who will give them a feeling of belonging. This is the basis of human existence, because it is in this coming together with another that a human being experiences love and, in that love, a sense of significance and meaning. Without love there is no life. Life has worth and fulfilment only when we can love and be loved.

People on a spiritual path accept and understand that their other half is God. Mystics, yogis and saints have created their spiritual lives through their union with God, whom they experience not only as their better half but as the One who is their All.

They have experienced how God, the eternal Beloved, fulfils all the desires of the heart. There is the sense of belonging eternally to a pure and faithful partner, the experience of giving and sharing what is most sacred and valued with each other. Complete wholeness permeates the life of one who feels that, having found God, they have found everything.

For the majority of people to fall in love with God seems difficult or even impossible. This is because our habit is to fall in love with a bodily being. With God, who has no physical image, it is difficult, because we cannot touch or hold Him. He seems too abstract, too distant. God is light – a point of light – so how can we fall in love with a point of light?

In mature relationships between human beings it is not the form we love but the qualities and personality of that person. A person may have beautiful eyes or a beautiful face but, after the initial attraction, the physical does not matter. What matters is what the person actually is – the person inside the physical costume. This is what creates and maintains the relationship.

If we understand God as a point of light, in the same way, it is not the form we love but the divine personality within that form: the pure qualities of love, peace and truth. When we experience these qualities, we feel overflowing happiness. We feel that this relationship between the Beloved and the lover is imperishable – a love that can never die.

God's love, unlike human love at this time, frees us from obligation, possessiveness and fear of loss. Godly love releases us from all limitations. True love always frees us from any and every form of negativity. The purer the love, the more mature is the relationship and, where there is maturity in a relationship, that relationship is beyond selfish motives. Each partner feels completely free.

In the love which human beings offer each other today there is rarely maturity or freedom. Of course, it was not always like this. Once, human love was selfless, but gradually it degenerated. Today only shadows remain and, because people believe in these shadows, it is rare to find a relationship which endures for any length of time. The experience of true relationship has been lost.

Love means loyalty in a relationship, the willingness to grow with the other and not easily to find fault and run away. Love is putting the beloved first in one's life, an act of constantly offering him or her the best. Love is to wish for and to give to the other, always putting the other first – before the self.

At this time in the world only God's love is that altruistic. Only He is ever-true and only a soul who is already true can be true to others. Love for God, the Supreme Soul, has the power to purify the soul. This releases the soul from the negative limitations imposed by ego and fear and teaches it to be true once more.

With true love there is only one word – 'yours'. The spiritual lover of the Beloved has such love that there is the deepest wish to transform totally and give everything to God. The soul knows that God will never exploit or damage it. God gives, guides and protects the soul's existence. God nourishes the soul with His Truth, strengthening it so that it can enjoy the real fruit of true life – happiness. Happiness comes from having the right relationship with ourselves and with other human beings.

God's love teaches us how to love ourselves and how to love others but, in order for us really to experience His love, God must be more than an abstract concept or a convenient social tradition. Only a real experience of God's love brings a positive transformation in behaviour and attitude.

Through history one finds that genuinely spiritual people have had such love for God that it has usually expressed itself in the desire to serve. If one loves, one gives.

The more one is complete, the more one is selfless. The experience of love from the Beloved completes us. We become self-sufficient but not self-centred.

It is God's love that makes us what we are. Love renews us and in this renewal there is the flowering of soul-consciousness.

Personal renewal through the love of the Beloved is possible when the heart is honest and when the Beloved is the priority in one's life. The mind can then easily become focused in the One. In the depths of this silent concentration the soul feels the bliss of union – not happiness but bliss. Happiness is what we experience through the physical senses, when the soul is in its body, playing its role as a human being. Bliss, however, is experienced when the soul, moving beyond the senses and anything physical, unites with God. Bliss is the union of soul and God through pure thought and pure feeling. Bliss is not possible between two human beings; love and happiness are, but not bliss. Bliss does not depend on, nor is governed by, anything of this physical world. It is beyond touch, sound, sight and time.

In bliss the soul enters the realm of the purest truth, the purest most sublime relationship possible between two beings. This is an experience only possible with and through God. In this union of bliss the soul feels eternity and knows that this relationship with the Beloved is blessed and deathless.

It is said in some traditions that the soul who remains in the bliss of Godly union miraculously transforms from a human into an angelic being: the supreme metamorphosis. Filled, sustained and moved by God's love, the angel serves humanity. The soul of an angel is beyond physical desires or attractions, all of which it knows would make it mortal. An angel's closeness to God makes it, like God, selfless and benevolent.

Reaching this stage of angelic consciousness is the proof that a human soul has truly made God the one and only Beloved.

God, the Friend

Friendship is probably the most valued of all relationships because a friend is totally our own choice. Parents and relatives are not chosen but given to us. That also has its own inherent value. However, a friend is someone who speaks to our heart, someone with whom we feel a magnetic affinity. When there is a mutual response between two people who are becoming friends, then a relationship can last a lifetime, or even beyond a lifetime!

Friendship is the coming together of equals. Even if there is a difference in abilities, roles or positions, there is a vision of equality which does not allow any feeling of either superiority or inferiority. This equality of vision permits a complete acceptance of one another. This creates closeness. There is such a respectful closeness that neither intrudes on the personality of the other, nor does either one harbour distaste for any weakness seen. Since the vision is unlimited, the true goodness of the other is always held as the measure of their reality. Weaknesses are seen as something foreign which, at the appropriate time, will make their exit.

Real friends can never divorce. There is a love which not only accommodates any shortcoming but actively transforms it with a word of encouragement, a smiling patience, an act of kindness. With a friend you do not have to prove yourself for you are loved and accepted for what you are, and what you are is enough. There is no need for any special achievements. All that a friend asks is that you be yourself.

A friend is a friend for all time, when there is a need for support or a moment of joy to share. Good times or bad, a friend is ever-present, ready to share, to serve, to listen or just to be there.

Friends always have a deep closeness to each other even if physically they are apart. This companionship conquers distance, time, and in fact, any kind of separation. Their mutual empathy is the basis of their communication. This communication is something more than just speaking; it is the ability to listen to the other's feelings, to tune one's self to the other's being. Such true communication allows for the purest interaction because there is a mirror of clarity where nothing can remain obscure. Nothing can be twisted or misunderstood.

Friendship means availability. A friend is available at all times and never says 'I don't have time', 'wait', 'later', or 'don't bother me now'. When there is need, a friend rushes to be there.

Every confidential word entrusted to a friend is sacred and sealed from the eyes and ears of others. Absolutely nothing would induce him or her to betray the friend's trust. Trust is an alliance between two hearts which have learnt through experience that this alliance can never be broken or betrayed. Trust dispels all fear of being misused or being abandoned.

God is the most trustworthy of friends. Unfortunately, this experience of God's friendship has been lost. Too often we are presented with the picture of God only as the Father and Judge. This is not a balanced or true picture at all, for God is also the Mother, the Beloved, the Teacher and the Guide, but especially He is our personal Friend and this friendship permeates all our other relationships with Him.

With God as a friend we can be open and know that in that openness there is a loyalty and an understanding of everything that is within our hearts. Though we have many other relationships with Him, He is always our Friend. This brings lightness and easiness to all our relationships with God.

It is said that a friend of God is a friend of all. Friendship with God teaches us and inspires us to be a true friend to others.

In true friendship there is respect and co-operation. This creates a unity essential for peaceful coexistence. A true friendship, but especially God's, is a blessing for eternity.

Silence

When silence is deep, brimming with fullness, when there is no more yearning for sound, when there is complete concentration on One, then thought, like an arrow, finds and melts into its target. There, the human soul not only glimpses God, but is also absorbed in the purity of that Being, totally, wholly and absolutely. Filled with the pure light that has now become its being, the soul radiates this energy as peace and love to others, a living lighthouse.

Silence is the bridge of communication between the Divine and the divine in the human. Silence is where we find what is most precious.

Spiritual silence is the positioning of the heart and mind in readiness for communication with the One.

It is not communication based on repetitive words, intellectual theories, nor asking for your

limited desires to be fulfilled. Sacred communication is the harmonising of the original self with
the Eternal One.

Spiritual silence gives us pure energy from the
Creative Source. Empowered, we burst out of
the cocoon of routine and the unlimited
horizons of a new vision open for us. To release
the self from negativity and routine, we require
silence. Absorbed in its depths, we are renewed.
In this renewal the mind clears itself, and grasps
a different perception of reality. The deepest
perception of all is of our own eternity.

The act of silence is as necessary for our spiritual
well being as breathing is for physical life.
Silence brings our mental and emotional energy
to a point of concentration, a point of stillness.
Without this inner stillness, we become like
puppets, pulled here and there by the many
different strings of external influences. This
inner point of stillness is the seed of autonomy,
which cuts the strings. The loss of energy ceases.

Silence heals. Silence is like a mirror. Everything
is clear. The mirror does not blame or criticise
but helps us to see things as they are, releasing us

from all types of wrong thinking. How does silence do this? Silence revives the original peace of the self – a peace that is innate, divine and, when invoked, ever-flowing, harmonising and healing every imbalance. Silence is full and it fills, gently, powerfully, consistently active.

To create silence, we step within. We connect with our eternal self, the soul. In that place of undisturbed tranquility, as if in a timeless womb, the process of renewal begins. There, a new pattern of pure energy is woven.

In this introspective space we reflect. We recollect what has been forgotten for a long time. We concentrate slowly and gently and as we do so, those original spiritual blueprints of love, truth and peace emerge and are experienced as personal and eternal realities. Through these, quality begins to enter life. The quality of something purer and truer in ourselves.

In silence, listening guides us into the right position, opening the channel of receptivity. Receptivity aligns us. A very necessary alignment, if we are truly to know and experience God. For receptivity we must clear ourself of ourself. We must stand clean, bare, simple, stripped of artificiality. Then genuine communication begins.

As we listen, we understand; as we understand, we reflect and gradually move into concentration. Concentration is when we are completely absorbed in one thought. Where there is love, concentration is natural and steady, like the still candle flame radiating its aura of light. The thought in which one is absorbed becomes one's world. When the human mind is absorbed in the thought of God, the person feels totally in union with Him. In this silent link of love, we awaken – not as part of an intellectual process, but as a state of being. This wakefulness is where we are fully conscious of Truth. Simultaneously we become conscious of the illusions in us and of the effort needed to remove them.

This wakefulness enables us to respond and receive what we would not normally notice, either on natural or supernatural levels. In the self, one becomes a truer being. Within silence, our subtle invisible rays of concentrated thought meet God.

This is the power of silence, which is often called 'meditation'. Sound cannot achieve this meeting with God. Sound, through song or chant, can only praise and glorify the closeness of union with the Divine but it cannot create it. Only silence creates the practical experience of union.

Concentrated silence is the wordless focus of pure attention on One. Love for that makes the focus easy and steady and fulfilling. This closeness of the self with the Supreme inevitably inspires the desire for change in the self; inspiration to better the self, to make the self worthy by fulfilling the original potential and, where one can, sharing the fruits of that realised potential with others.

In silence, the deepest orientation of consciousness is the desire to achieve personal perfection. This desire is a result of the divine flow of energy entering the human consciousness and inspiring belief in one's own worth. Personal perfection is accepted as being possible. It's the faith given by God as a gift to the soul. The possibility of perfection is accepted because the soul knows it is not alone in its effort; it has the constant support of Divine Love to achieve its goal.

In its connection with God, the soul becomes full. It feels itself to be complete, it has found what it was looking for. Divine Love works especially through silence; the soul is awakened from its sleep of ignorance and given new life, as in the story of Sleeping Beauty. The soul is the Sleeping Beauty, God is the prince and ignorance is the witch who casts her magic spell of slumber upon the princess. God's love for the soul is such that it is not stopped by any darkness or barrier but reaches the soul to awaken it, bringing it back to life, back to reality. Love breaks the iron spell.

It is through Love that I, as a soul, am awakened and am able to acknowledge my eternity. My reality is far more than my material appearance. My eternity is my reality. This is the truth of my existence. In Greek the word for truth is alithea which means 'not to forget'. The human being is under a very deep forgetfulness, an amnesia of spirit. We cannot achieve the awakened state, the true state of ourselves with our own skills of intellect. Attainment of Truth is not a matter of cleverness. We can only awaken when God helps us to remember. To remember is real knowing, it is Truth.

To achieve inner change, silence has to be love-filled not only peace filled. Many think that it is enough just to experience peace in the silence of meditation in order to achieve transformation of consciousness. Peace stabilises; peace harmonises and gently quietens. Peace lays the foundation. However, Love actively inspires; Love is the catalyst for change; Love moves the universe. Love moves all things towards their original freedom and happiness.

Both Peace and Love are needed. In their archetypal form, they both come from come from God, the Universal and immutable Source. It is this God-filled silence that restores human beings and this earth to their original state.

In silence, we realise that this silence is not only a return to the roots but, even more, it is a return to the seed, to the Beginning; it is a return to God, a return to the self, a return to right relationship.

Anthony Strano is the director of Brahma Kumaris in Athens, Greece. Born in Australia in 1951, he graduated from Macquarie University in Sydney with a Bachelor of Arts and a Diploma of Education.

A spiritual seeker all his life, Anthony became a student of the Brahma Kumaris in 1977. Now, years later, he is one of the Spiritual University's most dedicated and experienced teachers.

Over the years, he has travelled widely, sharing the knowledge he's gathered. He has run seminars and workshops throughout Europe and Australia on positive thinking and stress-free living, on education and values, on science and spirituality – in fact, on all areas of human development.

ABOUT THE BRAHMA KUMARIS WORLD SPIRITUAL UNIVERSITY

The Brahma Kumaris World Spiritual University is an international organisation working at all levels of society for positive change. Established in 1937 it now carries out a wide range of educational programmes for the development of human and spiritual values throughout its 4000 centres in over 70 countries.

The University is a non-governmental organisation in general consultative status with the Economic and Social Council of the United Nations and in consultative status with UNICEF. It is also the recipient of seven UN Peace Messenger awards.

Locally, centres provide courses and lectures in meditation and positive values, enabling individuals to recognise their true potential and make the most of their lives.

The University offers all its services free of charge.

Some of
THE BRAHMA KUMARIS CENTRES
in the United Kingdom and Ireland

London
Global Co-operation House, 65 Pound Lane, London NW10 2HH
Tel: 0181 727 3350
E-mail: london@bkwsu.com

Oxford
Global Retreat Centre, Nuneham Park
Nuneham Courtenay, Oxford OX44 9PG
Tel: 01865 343 551
E-mail: infoshare@bkwsugrc.demon.co.uk

Cardiff
8 Haxby Court, Felbridge Close, Atlantic Wharf, Cardiff Wales CF1 5BH
Tel: 01222 480 557

Edinburgh
20 Polwarth Crescent, Edinburgh, Scotland EH11 1HW
Tel: 0131 229 7220
E-mail: bkedinburgh@compuserve.com

Dublin
36 Lansdowne Road, Ballsbridge, Dublin 4, Ireland
Tel: 353 1 660 3967
E-mail: bknick@indigo.ie

Introductory courses in meditation are offered at each of our Centres throughout the country, free of charge.
For more information and the address of a centre near you,
Please contact one of the above centres.